Loving Partner
Journal

A Few Minutes A Day To A Deeper Connection

Thank you to our parents for your continual support
and for showing us what love looks like.

Loving Partner
Journal

A few minutes a day to a deeper connection

TO MY PARTNER:

LOVE:

This journal **heightens, nourishes, and ignites** the love we have for our partners through **gratitude, acts of kindness, and mindfulness.**

100 days, a **few minutes** a day, with fun activities along the way.

One book for you.
One book for your partner.
Grow together.

Reflect on the experience and exchange books at the end.

A **gift** unlike any other.

CONTENTS

LOVING DEEPLY

"So tell me, how deep is your love? Can it go deeper?" This question lights a fire inside me as the lyrics from Calvin Harris' "How Deep Is Your Love" play in the background, and it dangles an exhilarating challenge in front of us. Can we love each other more deeply? Can we plunge ourselves even deeper into this partnership, into this love, and light each other's souls on fire with the joy, passion, thrill, and immense growth that's possible in a relationship?

Yes, we can love deeper. We can become more loving partners and better partners—together. This is the essence of this book. We aim to help brighten your love. Whether it shines brightly like the sun or flickers dimly like an old light, there is always room for it to grow.

Committing ourselves to another person can be one of the most nourishing experiences of our lives; they can support our growth and bring out the best in us. This truth is best realized when we do more than just commit ourselves to a person and instead commit to learning how to love each other authentically, enabling that love to grow every day.

Whether you're currently in a strong, flourishing relationship, in a relationship that has seen its share of hardships, or anywhere in between, this journal is designed to bring partners together, deepening love one day at a time in just a few minutes a day. Through gratitude, acts of kindness, and mindfulness, we lay a strong foundation for partnerships, connecting in a way that intentionally heightens love. It's an exhilarating journey to love deeper by loving the simple details that make a partnership thrive.

Through the daily repetition of three simple, yet effective questions and weekly activities, you will super-charge your relationship, building a lasting, positive perception of each other and deepen your connection. Great change comes when these powerful tools— gratitude, acts of kindness, and mindfulness—become habits.

AUTHENTIC LOVE:
What Do We Want From Our Relationship?

Every relationship is wonderfully different; however, there are certain things that, when present in any relationship, help make it or break it.

We need to ask ourselves where our love is coming from. Is our love rooted in authenticity, or is it rooted in neediness? When our love is of a needy nature, we are looking for our partner to fulfil us, to provide a happiness/wholeness we feel we lack without that person. When we rely on another so strongly for our happiness, the weight of our world falls on their shoulders, and each action they take either helps to fulfil our needs or tears down the walls of our happiness. That is a lot of responsibility for us to place on our partner, and it can lead to a great deal of unnecessary disappointment and disputes. This kind of love is unsustainable and ultimately unhealthy.

When we switch to loving authentically, we recognize that our happiness is centred in ourselves and that we are responsible for our own well-being. This means that our love for our partner is no longer responsible for fulfilling a void in our life, but instead acknowledges that our journey through this life is improved because they are by our side—thus, invoking the true meaning of the word "partner."

This authentic love is what allows us to grow together as a couple and as individuals. Growth means that instead of holding onto a single idea of who our partner is, we support the discovery of new aspects of their being, and vice versa. Instead of entering each day as the couple we've always been, we enjoy the thrill of evolving into someone new and greater together each day. We struggle with growth when our love comes from a needy place because our image of our partner links directly to our well-being, and changing that image threatens us.

While growth may come with challenges, it also comes with great rewards. Challenges are amazing opportunities to build something stronger with our partner than what we had before, helping us improve how we see and treat each other.

This is where the *Loving Partner Journal* comes in. It helps us grow, strengthen, and deepen our connection. To build a strong foundation for relationships, we use three key principles.

1. **Gratitude:** When we are grateful for our partner, we are taking the time to really see them: who they are, who they are becoming, and all the good they do. This gratitude strengthens our relationship and primes us to appreciate our partner.

2. **Acts of kindness:** Taking action every day to show kindness to our partner is extremely powerful. By doing this, we are actively acknowledging that our actions matter, and we begin to take greater responsibility for our contributions to our partnership.

3. **Mindfulness:** When we actively bring present-moment awareness toward our partner's actions, we begin to really see all the ways they contribute to our lives and the lives of others. Mindfulness

allows us to feel the weight of how they add to our lives in small and large ways, so we can actively appreciate all they do.

When we do all three of these consciously daily, magic happens. Taking in the details helps us love authentically, helps us truly see our partner, and encourages us to love deeper than we ever have before. We hope this journal, these simple daily questions and weekly activities, will do just that: water growth, colour the details, weave together your lives, and nourish your relationship and soul.

WHY WE CREATED THIS JOURNAL

If fate exists, then it definitely had a hand in bringing the two of us together. For two people who claimed to not be looking for anything, we sure fell for each other hard. We met on a Halloween pub crawl. For weeks prior to the crawl, I (Lauren) had been searching for a Raphael Ninja Turtle costume but didn't find one that was quite right, so it was only fitting that the man of my dreams was out that night dressed as Raphael. We fell madly in love, unlike anything either of us had experienced before. We are now engaged, set to be married in 2018. Our relationship has been passionate; we've continually challenged each other to grow, and it's been filled with more love than we ever thought one person could feel for another—that soul-deep kind of connection.

Josh came up with the idea for the *Loving Partner Journal* one night while we were lying in bed talking. We had recently gotten engaged—promising that our lives would forever stay intertwined, that we would love each other forever. It's important to both of us that this love doesn't just last but that it continues to grow and inspire us to be and do our best. We want to not only make each other happy, but also continue to improve the love we are so grateful to have found.

Early on in a relationship, couples are really great at noticing all of the small things that they do for one another every day. In the early days of love, couples put time each day into being grateful, reflecting on what they've got, and doing things to make each other feel good. While our love has no doubt grown immeasurably since we first got together, we realized we weren't as attentive to those details as we had once been, and that it had been those details that kept us strong through different hardships we faced. We've had a number of challenges along the way, from spending three months apart near the start of our relationship to experiencing a large business failure together. Through this all, by recognizing, appreciating, and being there for each other, our relationship has continued to thrive. A strong foundation can withstand many trials. It was out of our desire to continue to strengthen our awareness and appreciation for each other that the *Loving Partner Journal* was born.

This journal brought us closer together and made us more thoughtful and more appreciative. The weekly activities kept us engaged, helping us find new ways to expand what we feel for each other. Most fun of all, exchanging our journals at the end made for a beautiful and emotional gift—to be able to see yourself through the eyes of someone who adores you is truly a treasure. We hope this journal can be a gift for your love too.

When we add gratitude, acts of kindness, and mindfulness to a relationship, magic happens and love deepens. The details of our day to day become part of a great love story. The familiar daily tasks that we take for granted become infused with passion as we act from a place a love. When we act from a place of love, our whole world begins to change.

Action creates change, and action from an authentic place of love infuses our world with love.

HOW TO MAKE
THE MOST OF
THIS JOURNAL

The *Loving Partner Journal* aims to give relationships the gift of a deeper connection for 100 days. Why 100 days? Because our partners deserve our commitment, and 100 days is long enough to help us build habits in our relationship that actually stick beyond that time period. Repetition is the key to success when looking to create lasting change. One hundred days is long enough to help us each feel the effect gratitude has on our personal lives too—gratitude has this beautiful way of spreading throughout our lives, when regularly used, to enhance all of our relationships.

Is it hard? We made it easy and simple to do. Just approach each day with honesty and explore new ways to show affection.

Do we need to see each other every day? Nope! Just think of your partner and put a little effort into connecting, whether it be a text, a call, an email, a tag on social media, or some other method. Not possible? Be creative in your answers for that day.

So how does the journal work? Glad you asked! Let's take a quick look at the whole process and then we'll break down each part, step by step. Each partner will fill out their own journal for 100 days. No peeking at your partner's journal during this time, as tempting as it may be—trust me, it's worth the wait. Start by filling out an intention for the journal, and then each day fill out three simple prompts, taking merely a few minutes a day. Easy peasy and it comes with a huge reward. Once a week there will be an activity that can be completed any time that week. This is a great way to take your relationship to new and exciting levels. When the 100 days are up, take some time to reflect and write a short letter to your love. Finally, switch journals! Read your love's letter and take a look through the day to day entries. Be prepared for your heart to melt and to gain a deeper understanding of your partner.

SETTING AN INTENTION

Setting an intention gives direction to our thoughts, consciously creating the desired outcome. To set an intention, we simply state what we would like to get out of the *Loving Partner Journal*. This is meant to be something we can achieve, not something we would like our partner to do for us. This is important because we are taking responsibility for our actions and are actively creating a direction for our actions day to day.

This is super powerful and can be used in all areas of our life to help us stay clear on what we want out of each situation we go into. We are putting the control and power into our own hands. When positive intentions are set, it helps us see each situation in a better light and primes our brain to foster a specific outcome.

By setting an intention, we have a statement to remind us each day of why we are committing to the *Loving Partner Journal*. Having a clearly defined "why," especially one that is emotionally charged, is not only powerful, but life changing too. Think of it as setting a heart goal, one that you feel deeply about … an intention that moves your mind, body, and soul. Make it personal.

Here are some examples. If one really speaks to you, feel free to use it, or create your own. The important thing is that we mean it and it resonates deeply on a heart level.

My Intention for the Loving Partner Journal is …

To feel grateful for my partner every day.

To show my partner just how deeply I love them and to learn new ways to express that love.

To fall back in love with the small details that make our relationship so special.

The possibilities are endless. Intentions help keep us on track and give us motivation to find the time to fill out our journal every day, because we've answered the important "why am I doing this" question.

DAILY PROMPTS

Here we reach the essence of the journal—the daily actions that have the power to shift the way we look at the love of our life. Each day we will be filling out these three simple prompts:

One reason I am grateful for my partner is …

One act of kindness I did for my partner today was …

One thing my partner has done for me or another today that I mindfully appreciate is …

Simple but so darn powerful when filled out with love and attention.

A great way to make this a priority is by picking one time of the day to fill it out. A reminder can even be set on our phones to make sure we remember. For example, we could choose to fill it out every day before bed or right after we get home from work. Pick a time that works for you!

Shortly, we'll take a close look at each question. First, here are sample pages from each of our books.

Lauren's Page:

One reason I am grateful for my partner is ...
How grounded and present Josh is.

One act of kindness I did for my partner today was ...
I made Josh tea.

One thing my partner has done for me or another today that I mindfully appreciate is ...
Josh got me the sweetest mug that says "I love you deerly" with a picture of a deer! So cute!

Josh's Page:

One reason I am grateful for my partner is ...
She loves to do things with me ☺

One act of kindness I did for my partner today was ...
Make veggies, bacon, and potatoes for breakfast.

One thing my partner has done for me or another today that I mindfully appreciate is ...
Danced with me in our room to Otto Knows—Not Alone.

As you can see, the answers don't have to be grand gestures of love; they can be whatever comes sincerely from your heart and mind! Answering honestly and from a place of love is the best way to get the most out of each day. Each day doesn't necessarily have to be a new answer. Some repetition may pop up over the 100 days, but the important thing is that each day is genuine and a reflection of what you experienced that day together. We loved using this book as a way to invent fun new things we could do for each other. It's both a great way to appreciate the everyday things we do for each other as well as explore diverse new ways we can add excitement to our day to day routines.

GRATITUDE FOR OUR PARTNER

Oh, gratitude, one of our favourite feelings ever! Gratitude is a rock star of a feeling because it not only helps us feel great about our world (i.e., whatever may be the object of our gratitude), but it also helps us feel personally full of goodness. It's a double whammy, an "I'm so grateful for this thing and that feels amazing" and a "my life is pretty great because I have this to be thankful for" combination. The simple daily act of feeling grateful adds so much richness to our lives, helping us really appreciate what we've got.

How awesome is it when we practice feeling grateful daily for our partner? It's pretty incredible. Our appreciation heightens every single day as we think about all of the amazing ways they add to our lives and to the lives of those around us. We have an excuse to ponder the reasons we fell for them in the first place, and a reason to pay attention to the traits that make them unique.

Gratitude can take many forms, big and small. We can be grateful for their actions, the things they say, their personality, the way they look, the way they make us feel, and their unique quirks. The possibilities are endless. We can equate "I'm grateful for" with "I love," "I like," "I appreciate," and "I'm thankful." We can think in any terms that help spark something meaningful inside us.

We can really benefit from this part of the *Loving Partner Journal* when we take time to feel the emotion connected to the thought. Putting emotion and thought together is such a strong way for us to create a lasting impact on the way we see the world around us, specifically the way we see our partner.

Not only will feeling gratitude for our partner improve our relationship with them, but it will also help improve the way we see the world, encouraging us to feel grateful more often throughout our day to day lives. We ingrain the neural pathway for gratitude through repetition, and this makes it easier and easier to feel gratitude daily. Pretty great, right?

Here are some examples from our books:

One reason I am grateful for my partner is ...
Lauren pushes me outside my comfort zone.
The way her hair flows through the breeze.
She supports me when I'm down.
Josh is always learning and sharing his knowledge with me.
The way he kisses me with so much love and care.
The way he connects with others and makes everyone feel so loved.

This section is all about being deeply personal and heartfelt. Here we listen to our hearts and how we feel. We practice being open and vulnerable throughout this book. We really get to connect and let our true feelings come forth.

PERFORMING ACTS OF KINDNESS FOR OUR PARTNER

Now for some fun and creativity. We get to do something (small or large) for our partner every day ... yay! What a joy, getting to express our love for the one we have decided to give our heart to. Acts of love and kindness come in many forms.

We read a great book together called *The 5 Love Languages* by Gary Chapman.[1] It's a wonderful book that really helped shape the way we think about showing love. Chapman discusses how we each have a "love tank" that, when full, leaves us feeling fulfilled, but when low can leave us feeling empty and drained. We each prefer to receive love in different ways, and there are certain kinds of love that we each tend to respond to the most. This type of love differs from person to person. By learning to speak our partner's love language, we can help ensure their love tank remains full, thus improving the quality of our relationship. The five love languages he outlines are:

Words of Affirmation
Quality Time
Receiving Gifts
Acts of Service
Physical Touch

We can aim to show our partner love in each of these love languages, having our acts of kindness fulfil a range of these categories over the 100 days. We can also take note of how our partner reacts to the different types of love and even have a conversation about what their primary and secondary love languages may be, as well as sharing our own. This is especially important because our partner's love language may differ from our own, which means taking the time to learn how we each prefer to receive love can help us connect in a way that is more meaningful to both partners. To better understand each love language, we highly recommend reading Chapman's book.

We all have the tendency to want to show love the way we like to receive love, but by finding out what makes our partner feel the most loved, we can make sure we're showing love in a way that speaks the strongest to them. We encourage showing a variety of different types of love from all of these categories. By identifying

---

1   Gary Chapman, *The 5 Love Languages* (Chicago: Northfield Publishing, 1992).

their main love languages, we can be sure to use these a bit more than the rest, so we always leave their love tank nice and full.

Going out of our way to perform acts of kindness helps to fill our hearts and our partner's heart too. What a win all around. These acts come in all shapes and sizes. The important thing is that they come from a place of love so that they are also enjoyable for us to perform.

Here are some examples of how to answer *One act of kindness I did for my partner today was ...* from each of the love language categories:

Words of Affirmation:
A compliment
Write a poem
Tell them one reason you love them

Quality Time:
Take a walk together
Ask about their day and listen without distractions
Eat a meal together without distractions

Acts of Service:
Make them coffee or tea
Wash the dishes
Take the kids to soccer practice so they can relax

Physical Touch:
Spend time cuddling
A shoulder massage
A long hug

Gifts:
Take them to dinner
Make something, like a homemade card
A small gift

And the list goes on! These are just some of the many ways we can show love for our partner every day through acts of kindness. From the small day to day things to a grand romantic gesture, they all count and are all appreciated. Through this practice, we are reminded of how much the small daily practices demonstrate our love and appreciation for each other.

MINDFULLY APPRECIATING OUR PARTNER'S ACTIONS

What is mindfulness, anyway? Mindfulness is the practice of actively bringing our attention to the present moment. Mindfulness means turning off auto-pilot to fully experience what is happening in the here and now. By focusing our attention on the present moment, we gain useful insight into our thoughts, emotions, and actions, as well as those of others. Mindfulness allows us to become involved in our present world. It gives us a new-found sense of control in our life because as our awareness of the present moment grows, we can practice stopping our automatic reactions and engage genuinely with our world, choosing thoughts and emotions that serve us and the world more lovingly. If we apply this definition of mindfulness to our partner, it means learning to be present in our relationship. We take ourselves off relationship auto-pilot, allowing ourselves to fully experience the joy of today, together. Our interactions become deeper because they are the reflection of thoughtful, emotive choice instead of automatic reaction.

Here we mindfully practice the art of noticing what our partner does for us and others, appreciating actions of all sizes. The goal here is to use mindfulness to really see all of the wonderful ways they contribute to this world, and then express that recognition in the form of appreciation. We can also embrace new experiences, thinking of the five love languages and acknowledging actions we may have missed before.

By paying mindful attention to our partner's actions, we can ask ourselves whether we've been holding on to any unfair biases, not truly recognizing the full extent of how our partner contributes to our relationship. This may manifest as a belief that we are always doing "more" in the relationship, when in reality we may simply be contributing in different ways. This bias may also present itself because it's often easier to recall the work we have personally done over that of our partner. Mindful awareness of our partner's actions, combined with appreciation, is a great way to provide credit where credit is due. It also feels amazing to be appreciated. This action alone naturally increases the amount each partner is willing to contribute because love exists on both ends of the giving and receiving sides when mindful appreciation is present.

With this section, we mindfully and lovingly put effort into noticing the different ways our partner shows us and others love. This is a time for genuine appreciation for their actions. Genuine appreciation means avoiding backhanded attacks like "I appreciate how they finally did the dishes for once." This accomplishes nothing and takes away from the practice. Flipping that example to "I appreciate how they did the dishes after dinner so I could relax" displays genuine appreciation. When we mindfully appreciate our partner, we let their good acts shine and stand as an example of how they care.

By practicing mindful appreciation, we get to see all the ways our partner brings love and kindness into the world for us and for others. This experience can be a lot of fun and makes us feel proud to have such an amazing partner.

Here are some of our examples:

One thing my partner has done for me or another today that I mindfully appreciate is ...
She said "thank you for the ride."
She made my dad's birthday special for him.
Let me eat the rest of the cookie batter.

Today Josh gave me a bookmark.

How he changes the lives of the clients he trains. A client gave him a thank you frame today.

He waited for my mom to pick me up so he could say hi.

And with this, we have beautifully come full circle. We practice gratitude, contribute to our partner's life with acts of kindness, and mindfully appreciate how they contribute to our lives and the lives of those around us. Practicing our vulnerability with these acts, opening emotionally, and investing into one another, we give ourselves the gift of full hearts.

WEEKLY ACTIVITIES

The weekly activities are designed to add a little spice and fun into our weeks. Over the course of the 100 days, the activities cover all of the love languages and help us practice connecting in new ways. What's wonderful about this is that it encourages us to get out of our comfort zone, learn different ways we can make our partner happy, and figure out if there are types of activities that really mean a lot to us too! The important thing is that even if an activity feels uncomfortable, we still give it our all and complete it as sincerely as possible, knowing that in doing so we deepen our connection with our partners. Each week will also include a variation for long distance partners because distance doesn't limit growth or joy. Have fun!

THE FINAL LETTER AND JOURNAL EXCHANGE

And now for our favourite part. We get excited just thinking about it, and love, love, love knowing the joy that will come out of this exchange!

After 100 days of growing and deepening love, it is time to bring the whole experience together. Take time to flip through your journal; read over a number of pages. Really soak the experience in and reflect. Here we ask ourselves what we learned from this experience. What does our partner mean to us? How do they enrich our lives? What did gratitude, acts of kindness, and mindfulness teach us about what it means to be in a partnership? How did our concept of love expand?

Thinking about our partner and this experience from many different directions, and tapping into the thoughts and emotions that sum it up, it is time to write a short letter to our love. This letter is an expression of whatever is in your heart, whatever you want your partner to know about how you feel. It's truly a beautiful experience to put this growth and love into words. Allow yourself to speak genuinely, be vulnerable, and give with words. The letter can be any length. We left a few pages at the end. The letter can fill them all or be shorter, as long as it's an honest expression of our feelings.

When both partners are done their letters, exchange journals! Read the letter and look through the pages. Bask in the truth of their expression. Read their journal non-judgementally and with an open heart. Know that what your partner wrote is what makes them feel loved and what they love about you. Their journal is an expression of their desire to grow together, to love authentically.

Let their words carry you to new heights.

SHARING THE LOVE

When we allow love into our lives, it has the potential to change the world. Love, happiness, and growth in our partnerships translate to happiness in other areas of our life, encouraging us to look at the world through another lens.

Practicing gratitude, acts of kindness, and mindfulness with the person we hold close to our heart makes it easy to practice the same with friends, family, acquaintances, and even strangers. Love in our heart acts like a ripple from a stone thrown into a pond. It grows larger and larger and affects everything surrounding it. We can shine this love and watch it overflow, helping us grow mind, body, and soul and helping us change the world.

Let's not hold back; let's shine our love and use these practices not only with our partner (beyond the 100 days), but also unconditionally with the people who cross our paths, knowing that the energy of love will help create changes in their life too.

If you find this practice helps your partnership flourish, we encourage you to please tell others about this book. Please recommend it and write a review; we would be very grateful. Sharing what we've found useful with others is a great way to spread joy in this beautiful life. It's our goal to help as many partners as possible strengthen their bonds, and we can't do it alone. Your support is greatly appreciated.

We would also love to see and hear how it's going for you! Post a picture of you and your journal on Instagram and Facebook, tagging us @lovingpartnerjournal and using the hashtag #lovingpartnerjournal. It's so much fun to see how we're all on this journey together! The world can always use more love!

WISHING YOU HAPPINESS, LOVE, AND GROWTH

We hope that you have as much fun with this journal as we did! Our partner plays such an important role in our life as we take this journey together. The quality of this relationship is a huge game changer and, for us, this practice helped strengthen our bond and helped our love grow to new depths. We learned a lot about ourselves, our relationship, and each other. We wish the same to you. May this journey help you look at your connection and love in a new way, and may it breed happiness in your lives. It may even become an annual activity! Sending so much love from our partnership to yours, xo.

Loving Partner
Journal

A few minutes a day to a deeper connection

MY INTENTION

"In order to carry a positive action,
we must develop here a positive vision."
Dalai Lama

My intention for the Loving Partner Journal is …

_____

_____

_____

_____

• DAY 1 •

Love Deeply

One reason I am grateful for my partner is …

_____

_____

_____

One act of kindness I did for my partner today was …

_____

_____

_____

One thing my partner has done for me or another today that I mindfully appreciate is …

_____

_____

_____

"You never lose by loving. You always lose by holding back."
Barbara de Angelis

· DAY 2 ·

Love Authentically

One reason I am grateful for my partner is ...

_____

_____

_____

One act of kindness I did for my partner today was ...

_____

_____

_____

One thing my partner has done for me or another today that I mindfully appreciate is ...

_____

_____

_____

"Positive anything is better than negative nothing."
Elbert Hubbard

WEEKLY ACTIVITY #1

OLD PHOTO DATE!
"Flashback"

Spend some time going through old photos together. These can be photos from when you were young (childhood, adolescence) or photos from throughout your time dating each other. It's a great chance to reminisce, maybe learn some new things about each other, and reconnect over past events. Both partners should contribute pictures. If someone doesn't have pictures to share, share old stories instead! Spend fifteen to thirty-plus minutes together.

Long Distance: the activity remains the same. Connect for a call or facetime/skype, send photos to each other and share stories.

Date: _____

• DAY 3 •

Weekly Activity: Flashback

One reason I am grateful for my partner is ...

_____

_____

_____

One act of kindness I did for my partner today was ...

_____

_____

_____

One thing my partner has done for me or another today that I mindfully appreciate is ...

_____

_____

_____

"You simply will not be the same two months from now after consciously giving thanks each and every day for the abundance that exists in your life. And you will set in motion an ancient spiritual law: the more you have and are grateful for, the more will be given to you."
Sarah Ban Breathnach

· DAY 4 ·

Weekly Activity: Flashback

One reason I am grateful for my partner is ...

_____

_____

_____

One act of kindness I did for my partner today was ...

_____

_____

_____

One thing my partner has done for me or another today that I mindfully appreciate is ...

_____

_____

_____

"I saw that you were perfect, and so I loved you.
Then I saw that you were not perfect and I loved you even more."
Angelita Lim

• DAY 5 •

Weekly Activity: Flashback

One reason I am grateful for my partner is …

_____

_____

_____

One act of kindness I did for my partner today was …

_____

_____

_____

One thing my partner has done for me or another today that I mindfully appreciate is …

_____

_____

_____

*"When we choose not to focus on what is missing from our lives but are grateful for the abundance that is present …
we experience heaven on earth."*
Sarah Ban Breathnach

· DAY 6 ·

Weekly Activity: Flashback

One reason I am grateful for my partner is ...

_____

_____

_____

One act of kindness I did for my partner today was ...

_____

_____

_____

One thing my partner has done for me or another today that I mindfully appreciate is ...

_____

_____

_____

> *"The most important thing in life is to learn*
> *how to give out love, and to let it come in."*
> *Morrie Schwartz*

Date: _____

• DAY 7 •

One reason I am grateful for my partner is ...

_____

_____

_____

One act of kindness I did for my partner today was ...

_____

_____

_____

One thing my partner has done for me or another today that I mindfully appreciate is ...

_____

_____

_____

"Everywhere you go is a chance to change the world. One smile, one hug, one act of kindness can make the world of difference to someone!"
Karen Salmansohn

• DAY 8 •

Weekly Activity: Flashback

One reason I am grateful for my partner is ...

_____

_____

_____

One act of kindness I did for my partner today was ...

_____

_____

_____

One thing my partner has done for me or another today that I mindfully appreciate is ...

_____

_____

_____

> "Life is like a coin. You can spend it any way you wish,
> but you only spend it once."
> Lillian Dickson

• DAY 9 •

Weekly Activity: Flashback

One reason I am grateful for my partner is …

_____

_____

_____

One act of kindness I did for my partner today was …

_____

_____

_____

One thing my partner has done for me or another today that I mindfully appreciate is …

_____

_____

_____

"If you have made mistakes, there is always another chance for you. You may have a fresh start any moment you choose, for this thing we call 'failure' is not the falling down, but the staying down."
Mary Pickford

WEEKLY ACTIVITY #2

WRITING EXPERIENCE!
"I Feel Loved When …"

Write a paragraph about what makes you feel loved and take turns sharing. Spend time thinking about the moments you feel the most loved. What kind of activities or actions signify love to you? Reflect on the five love languages we talked about in the section "How to Make the Most of This Journal: Performing Act of Kindness for Our Partner." Do you feel more loved by one or two of these love languages than the others? Your goal here is to get to know yourself a little deeper so you can help your partner understand what makes you happy and what makes you feel loved. This is important because you may each receive love in different ways, so this can help you show and receive love in a way that makes an impact on each of you specifically. Once you are both done your paragraphs, take turns reading them to each other. Listen with an open mind and an open heart, knowing your partner is giving you the key to their love.

Long Distance: the activity remains the same.

· DAY 10 ·

Weekly Activity: I Feel Loved When …

One reason I am grateful for my partner is …

_____

_____

_____

One act of kindness I did for my partner today was …

_____

_____

_____

One thing my partner has done for me or another today that I mindfully appreciate is …

_____

_____

_____

"Without communication there is no relationship. Without respect there is no love. Without trust there is no reason to continue."
Unknown

Date: _____

• DAY 11 •

One reason I am grateful for my partner is …

_____

_____

_____

One act of kindness I did for my partner today was …

_____

_____

_____

One thing my partner has done for me or another today that I mindfully appreciate is …

_____

_____

_____

"Your task is not to seek for love, but merely to seek and find all the barriers within yourself that you have built against it."
Rumi

• DAY 12 •

Weekly Activity: I Feel Loved When …

One reason I am grateful for my partner is …

_____

_____

_____

One act of kindness I did for my partner today was …

_____

_____

_____

One thing my partner has done for me or another today that I mindfully appreciate is …

_____

_____

_____

"What if you gave someone a gift, and they neglected to thank you for it—would you be likely to give them another? Life is the same way. In order to attract more of the blessings that life has to offer, you must truly appreciate what you already have."
Ralph Marston

• DAY 13 •

Weekly Activity: I Feel Loved When …

One reason I am grateful for my partner is …

_____

_____

_____

One act of kindness I did for my partner today was …

_____

_____

_____

One thing my partner has done for me or another today that I mindfully appreciate is …

_____

_____

_____

"Gratitude unlocks the fullness of life. It turns what we have into enough, and more. It can turn a meal into a feast, a house into a home, a stranger into a friend."
Melody Beattie

Date: _____

• DAY 14 •

Weekly Activity: I Feel Loved When ...

One reason I am grateful for my partner is ...

_____

_____

_____

One act of kindness I did for my partner today was ...

_____

_____

_____

One thing my partner has done for me or another today that I mindfully appreciate is ...

_____

_____

_____

"Know the wholeness, perfection and beauty that you are. Learn to rest in that place within you that is your true home. Find the love you seek, by first finding the love within yourself."
Ravi Shankar

Date: _____

• DAY 15 •

Weekly Activity: I Feel Loved When ...

One reason I am grateful for my partner is ...

_____

_____

_____

One act of kindness I did for my partner today was ...

_____

_____

_____

One thing my partner has done for me or another today that I mindfully appreciate is ...

_____

_____

_____

"Forgiveness does not change the past, but it does enlarge the future."
Paul Boese

· DAY 16 ·

Weekly Activity: I Feel Loved When …

One reason I am grateful for my partner is …

_____

_____

_____

One act of kindness I did for my partner today was …

_____

_____

_____

One thing my partner has done for me or another today that I mindfully appreciate is …

_____

_____

_____

"In daily life we must see that it is not happiness that makes us grateful, but gratefulness that makes us happy."
David Steindl-Rast

WEEKLY ACTIVITY #3

HAVE SOME FUN!
"Smile Time"

This week, the goal is to plan a fun activity together. Find a reason to laugh out loud together. Laughter is a great way to really connect, feel great, and grow closer. Some fun ideas are watching a comedy show (go to a show or find one online), play a game, or try something new and silly together. Laughing together a little bit every day can add so much joy to your partnership, so have fun planning an activity and let the energy from this time together carry over, becoming an inspiration for magic day to day.

Long Distance: distance can't hold back laughter. Connect for a call, or facetime/skype and do an activity together that will make you smile. This could be telling a funny story, playing a game, watching something funny together, etc.!

Date: _____

• DAY 17 •

Weekly Activity: Smile Time

One reason I am grateful for my partner is …

_____

_____

_____

One act of kindness I did for my partner today was …

_____

_____

_____

One thing my partner has done for me or another today that I mindfully appreciate is …

_____

_____

_____

> *"It is not a lack of love, but a lack of friendship*
> *that makes unhappy marriages."*
> Friedrich Nietzsche

• DAY 18 •

Weekly Activity: Smile Time

One reason I am grateful for my partner is ...

_____

_____

_____

One act of kindness I did for my partner today was ...

_____

_____

_____

One thing my partner has done for me or another today that I mindfully appreciate is ...

_____

_____

_____

"Promise me you'll always remember: You're braver than you believe, and stronger than you seem, and smarter than you think."
A. A. Milne

51

· DAY 19 ·

Weekly Activity: Smile Time

One reason I am grateful for my partner is ...

_____

_____

_____

One act of kindness I did for my partner today was ...

_____

_____

_____

One thing my partner has done for me or another today that I mindfully appreciate is ...

_____

_____

_____

"I've learned that people will forget what you said, people will forget what you did, but people will never forget how you made them feel."
Maya Angelou

• DAY 20 •

Weekly Activity: Smile Time

One reason I am grateful for my partner is ...

_____

_____

_____

One act of kindness I did for my partner today was ...

_____

_____

_____

One thing my partner has done for me or another today that I mindfully appreciate is ...

_____

_____

_____

"You don't love someone for their looks, or their clothes, or for their fancy car, but because they sing a song only you can hear."
Oscar Wilde

• DAY 21 •

Weekly Activity: Smile Time

One reason I am grateful for my partner is …

_____

_____

_____

One act of kindness I did for my partner today was …

_____

_____

_____

One thing my partner has done for me or another today that I mindfully appreciate is …

_____

_____

_____

> *"Don't wait for your feelings to change before you take action.*
> *Take the action and your feelings will change."*
> Barbara Baron

Date: _____

• DAY 22 •

Weekly Activity: Smile Time

One reason I am grateful for my partner is ...

_____

_____

_____

One act of kindness I did for my partner today was ...

_____

_____

_____

One thing my partner has done for me or another today that I mindfully appreciate is ...

_____

_____

_____

"A journey of a thousand miles begins with a single step."
Lao Tse

55

· DAY 23 ·

Weekly Activity: Smile Time

One reason I am grateful for my partner is …

_____

_____

_____

One act of kindness I did for my partner today was …

_____

_____

_____

One thing my partner has done for me or another today that I mindfully appreciate is …

_____

_____

_____

*"Being deeply loved by someone gives you strength
while loving someone deeply gives you courage."*
Lao Tzu

WEEKLY ACTIVITY #4

INTIMATE LOVING TOUCH!
"Close and Cuddly"

Spend thirty minutes cuddling and enjoying being close. Block out some time for each other, set the mood (candles, music, etc.), and enjoy being in each other's presence. For this thirty minutes, being close is all that matters. Instead of sexual touch, let the goal here be intimate, loving touch without any sort of agenda aside from loving, physical connection. This is a great way to let your partner know they are safe with you and to feel that you are safe with them. Practicing intimacy is an incredible way to dive deeper into our capacity for love.

Long Distance: set the mood and practice talking intimately to each other. Create your own style of intimacy. This can include: sharing what you feel, sharing thoughts of each other, what you enjoy about each other, what you miss, and much more.

• DAY 24 •

Weekly Activity: Close and Cuddly

One reason I am grateful for my partner is ...

_____

_____

_____

One act of kindness I did for my partner today was ...

_____

_____

_____

One thing my partner has done for me or another today that I mindfully appreciate is ...

_____

_____

_____

"When two people in an intimate-couple relationship look at their interactions as opportunities to learn about themselves instead of change each other, they are infusing their relationship with the energy of spiritual partnership."
Gary Zukav

• DAY 25 •

One reason I am grateful for my partner is ...

_____

_____

_____

One act of kindness I did for my partner today was ...

_____

_____

_____

One thing my partner has done for me or another today that I mindfully appreciate is ...

_____

_____

_____

"What wisdom can you find that is greater than kindness?"
Jean-Jacques Rousseau

• DAY 26 •

Weekly Activity: Close and Cuddly

One reason I am grateful for my partner is ...

_____

_____

_____

One act of kindness I did for my partner today was ...

_____

_____

_____

One thing my partner has done for me or another today that I mindfully appreciate is ...

_____

_____

_____

"Nothing ever goes away until it has taught us what we need to know."
Pema Chödrön

Date: _____

• DAY 27 •

One reason I am grateful for my partner is …

_____

_____

_____

One act of kindness I did for my partner today was …

_____

_____

_____

One thing my partner has done for me or another today that I mindfully appreciate is …

_____

_____

_____

"Love liberates. It doesn't bind."
Maya Angelou

Date: _____

• DAY 28 •

Weekly Activity: Close and Cuddly

One reason I am grateful for my partner is ...

_____

_____

_____

One act of kindness I did for my partner today was ...

_____

_____

_____

One thing my partner has done for me or another today that I mindfully appreciate is ...

_____

_____

_____

> *"There's no beauty that you could perceive or create*
> *if it were not already within you."*
> Peter Shepherd

Date: _____

• DAY 29 •

One reason I am grateful for my partner is ...

_____

_____

_____

One act of kindness I did for my partner today was ...

_____

_____

_____

One thing my partner has done for me or another today that I mindfully appreciate is ...

_____

_____

_____

> *"Love takes off masks that we fear we cannot live without*
> *and know we cannot live within."*
> James A. Baldwin

63

· DAY 30 ·

Weekly Activity: Close and Cuddly

One reason I am grateful for my partner is ...

_____

_____

_____

One act of kindness I did for my partner today was ...

_____

_____

_____

One thing my partner has done for me or another today that I mindfully appreciate is ...

_____

_____

_____

"The time is always right to do what is right."
Martin Luther King

WEEKLY ACTIVITY #5

GET PHYSICAL!
"Fit Fun"

Find a physical activity to do together this week. For example, go on a hike, go for a walk, take an exercise class, do an at-home yoga video on YouTube, try indoor rock climbing, go for a bike ride, or if it's winter, go ice skating or skiing. The possibilities are endless. Physical activities with our partner are a win-win. We spend time connecting and look after our health at the same time. Bonus—physical exercise has been shown to release feel-good endorphins, giving us a happiness boost! If this is already a regular in your routine, try something new.

If doing something physical isn't possible because of physical limitations, spend some quality time together in nature, soaking in its beauty!

Long Distance: find a similar activity you each can do and spend time connecting after to share all the details of the experience, or chat while both taking a walk/doing an activity.

• DAY 31 •

One reason I am grateful for my partner is ...

_____

_____

_____

One act of kindness I did for my partner today was ...

_____

_____

_____

One thing my partner has done for me or another today that I mindfully appreciate is ...

_____

_____

_____

> *"Life's challenges are not supposed to paralyze you,*
> *they are supposed to help you discover who you are."*
> Bernice Johnson Reagon

Date: _____

• DAY 32 •

> **Weekly Activity:** Fit Fun

One reason I am grateful for my partner is ...

_____

_____

_____

One act of kindness I did for my partner today was ...

_____

_____

_____

One thing my partner has done for me or another today that I mindfully appreciate is ...

_____

_____

_____

"Keep love in your heart. A life without it is like a sunless garden when the flowers are dead. The consciousness of loving and being loved brings a warmth and a richness to life that nothing else can bring."
Oscar Wilde

· DAY 33 ·

Weekly Activity: Fit Fun

One reason I am grateful for my partner is ...

_____

_____

_____

One act of kindness I did for my partner today was ...

_____

_____

_____

One thing my partner has done for me or another today that I mindfully appreciate is ...

_____

_____

_____

"Your living is determined not so much by what life brings to you as by the attitude you bring to life; not so much by what happens to you as by the way your mind looks at what happens."
Kahlil Gibran

Date: _____

• DAY 34 •

One reason I am grateful for my partner is ...

_____

_____

_____

One act of kindness I did for my partner today was ...

_____

_____

_____

One thing my partner has done for me or another today that I mindfully appreciate is ...

_____

_____

_____

"I choose… to live by choice, not by chance; to make changes, not excuses; to be motivated, not manipulated; to be useful, not used; to excel, not compete. I choose self-esteem, not self pity. I choose to listen to my inner voice, not the random opinion of others."
Unknown

Date: _____

· DAY 35 ·

Weekly Activity: Fit Fun

One reason I am grateful for my partner is …

_____

_____

_____

One act of kindness I did for my partner today was …

_____

_____

_____

One thing my partner has done for me or another today that I mindfully appreciate is …

_____

_____

_____

"*I swear I couldn't love you more than I do right now,
and yet I know I will tomorrow.*"
Leo Christopher

• DAY 36 •

Weekly Activity: Fit Fun

One reason I am grateful for my partner is ...

_____

_____

_____

One act of kindness I did for my partner today was ...

_____

_____

_____

One thing my partner has done for me or another today that I mindfully appreciate is ...

_____

_____

_____

"Before you speak, think: Is it necessary? Is it true? Is it kind?
Will it hurt anyone? Will it improve on the silence?"
Sri Sathya Sai Baba

· DAY 37 ·

Weekly Activity: Fit Fun

One reason I am grateful for my partner is ...

_____

_____

_____

One act of kindness I did for my partner today was ...

_____

_____

_____

One thing my partner has done for me or another today that I mindfully appreciate is ...

_____

_____

_____

> *"We awaken in others the same attitude of mind*
> *we hold towards them."*
> *Elbert Hubbard*

WEEKLY ACTIVITY #6

LOVING EXCHANGE!
"Small Gift, Big Love"

Give your partner a small but thoughtful gift this week. It can be homemade (a card, a painting, a poem, etc.), something you find (a flower, a pretty stone, etc.), or something purchased under $20. Put some thought into it and get creative. Pick something that'll put a smile on your partner's face, and have fun gratefully receiving too. A relationship is equally about giving and receiving. Our relationship flourishes when we are willing to put into the relationship just as much as we are open to receiving the love our partner has to offer.

Long Distance: you can send your partner a gift under $20, make them something online, draw a picture, send a photo, or whatever your heart desires.

Date: _____

• DAY 38 •

Weekly Activity: Small Gift, Big Love

One reason I am grateful for my partner is ...

_____

_____

_____

One act of kindness I did for my partner today was ...

_____

_____

_____

One thing my partner has done for me or another today that I mindfully appreciate is ...

_____

_____

_____

"To be brave is to love someone unconditionally,
without expecting anything in return."
Madonna

• DAY 39 •

> **Weekly Activity:** Small Gift, Big Love

One reason I am grateful for my partner is …

_____

_____

_____

One act of kindness I did for my partner today was …

_____

_____

_____

One thing my partner has done for me or another today that I mindfully appreciate is …

_____

_____

_____

"How wonderful it is that nobody need wait a single moment before starting to improve the world."
Anne Frank

Date: _____

• DAY 40 •

Weekly Activity: Small Gift, Big Love

One reason I am grateful for my partner is ...

_____

_____

_____

One act of kindness I did for my partner today was ...

_____

_____

_____

One thing my partner has done for me or another today that I mindfully appreciate is ...

_____

_____

_____

"Love is friendship on fire."
Unknown

Date: _____

• DAY 41 •

Weekly Activity: Small Gift, Big Love

One reason I am grateful for my partner is ...

_____

_____

_____

One act of kindness I did for my partner today was ...

_____

_____

_____

One thing my partner has done for me or another today that I mindfully appreciate is ...

_____

_____

_____

"Each moment of life is only as precious as is our ability to attend to it."
Guy Finley

· DAY 42 ·

Weekly Activity: Small Gift, Big Love

One reason I am grateful for my partner is ...

_____

_____

_____

One act of kindness I did for my partner today was ...

_____

_____

_____

One thing my partner has done for me or another today that I mindfully appreciate is ...

_____

_____

_____

"Love is how it feels to recognize our essential unity. Knowing you are one with all, you find yourself in love with all."
Timothy Freke

• DAY 43 •

Weekly Activity: Small Gift, Big Love

One reason I am grateful for my partner is ...

_____

_____

_____

One act of kindness I did for my partner today was ...

_____

_____

_____

One thing my partner has done for me or another today that I mindfully appreciate is ...

_____

_____

_____

"The smallest change in perspective can transform a life.
What tiny attitude adjustment might turn your world around?"
Oprah Winfrey

Date: _____

• DAY 44 •

Weekly Activity: Small Gift, Big Love

One reason I am grateful for my partner is ...

_____

_____

_____

One act of kindness I did for my partner today was ...

_____

_____

_____

One thing my partner has done for me or another today that I mindfully appreciate is ...

_____

_____

_____

"Nirvana or enlightenment or true spiritual growth can be achieved only through persistent exercise of real love."
M. Scott Peck

WEEKLY ACTIVITY #7

EYE GAZING!
"Soul Stare"

This week, the activity is two minutes of continuous eye gazing. They say the eyes are the seat of our soul. Eye gazing is a beautifully intimate activity that helps connect people at a deep level and can aid in dissolving barriers and creating more comfort between individuals. Every experience is extremely unique. Feel free to try it more than once.

To eye gaze, sit at a comfortable distance from one another. Get comfortable. Set a timer and begin gazing into each other's eyes for two minutes. During this time, refrain from talking and touching. Simply look. When the time is up, take a second to relax your eyes and reflect personally on the experience. Do whatever comes naturally next—laugh, cry, embrace, talk about your experience, or move forward with your day. Enjoy the few minutes of deep connection.

Long Distance: thankfully technology makes it easy to see each other no matter the distance so the activity remains the same.

· DAY 45 ·

> **Weekly Activity:** Soul Stare

One reason I am grateful for my partner is ...

_____

_____

_____

One act of kindness I did for my partner today was ...

_____

_____

_____

One thing my partner has done for me or another today that I mindfully appreciate is ...

_____

_____

_____

"Only as high as I reach can I grow, only as far as I seek can I go, only as deep as I look can I see, only as much as I dream can I be."
Karen Ravn

• DAY 46 •

Weekly Activity: Soul Stare

One reason I am grateful for my partner is ...

_____

_____

_____

One act of kindness I did for my partner today was ...

_____

_____

_____

One thing my partner has done for me or another today that I mindfully appreciate is ...

_____

_____

_____

"Love is always patient and kind. It is never jealous. Love is never boastful or conceited. It is never rude or selfish. It does not take offense and is not resentful. Love takes no pleasure in other people's sins, but delights in the truth. It is always ready to excuse, to trust, to hope, and to endure whatever comes."
1 Corinthians 13:4–7

Date: _____

• DAY 47 •

Weekly Activity: Soul Stare

One reason I am grateful for my partner is ...

_____

_____

_____

One act of kindness I did for my partner today was ...

_____

_____

_____

One thing my partner has done for me or another today that I mindfully appreciate is ...

_____

_____

_____

> *"Trust is the glue of life. It's the most essential ingredient in effective communication. It's the foundational principle that holds all relationships."*
> Stephen R. Covey

84

Date: _____

• DAY 48 •

One reason I am grateful for my partner is ...

_____

_____

_____

One act of kindness I did for my partner today was ...

_____

_____

_____

One thing my partner has done for me or another today that I mindfully appreciate is ...

_____

_____

_____

"In order to heal we must first forgive ...
and sometimes the person we must forgive is ourselves."
Mila Bron

· DAY 49 ·

Weekly Activity: Soul Stare

One reason I am grateful for my partner is ...

_____

_____

_____

One act of kindness I did for my partner today was ...

_____

_____

_____

One thing my partner has done for me or another today that I mindfully appreciate is ...

_____

_____

_____

"Never speak out of anger, never act out of fear, never choose from impatience, but wait ... and peace will appear."
Guy Finley

• DAY 50 •

Weekly Activity: Soul Stare

One reason I am grateful for my partner is ...

_____

_____

_____

One act of kindness I did for my partner today was ...

_____

_____

_____

One thing my partner has done for me or another today that I mindfully appreciate is ...

_____

_____

_____

"The salvation of man is through love and in love."
Victor Frankl

• DAY 51 •

Weekly Activity: Soul Stare

One reason I am grateful for my partner is ...

_____

_____

_____

One act of kindness I did for my partner today was ...

_____

_____

_____

One thing my partner has done for me or another today that I mindfully appreciate is ...

_____

_____

_____

*"The ultimate measure of a man is not where he stands
in moments of comfort and convenience, but where he stands
at times of challenge and controversy."*
Martin Luther King

WEEKLY ACTIVITY #8

QUALITY TIME!
"Date Night"

Date night fun! Plan a great night together for quality time, just the two of you. Challenge your routines and plan something out of the ordinary. If you're always going out, plan a nice night in. If you're always staying in, have a nice night out. Consider trying something new! Planning date nights is a great way to keep the relationship fresh and to maintain the spark of the dating stage. It's important partners take time for one another, and a date night is the perfect setting to make each other feel special.

Long Distance: come up with a creative new way to spend a night together despite the distance. This could include: playing a game together online, watching a movie together, sharing some wine while talking, listening to a playlist together, and more.

Date: _____

• DAY 52 •

One reason I am grateful for my partner is ...

_____

_____

_____

One act of kindness I did for my partner today was ...

_____

_____

_____

One thing my partner has done for me or another today that I mindfully appreciate is ...

_____

_____

_____

> *"It is possible to experience an awakening in this life through realizing just how precious each moment, each mental process, and each breath truly is."*
> Christy Turlington

90

• DAY 53 •

Weekly Activity: Date Night

One reason I am grateful for my partner is ...

_____

_____

_____

One act of kindness I did for my partner today was ...

_____

_____

_____

One thing my partner has done for me or another today that I mindfully appreciate is ...

_____

_____

_____

"We accept the love we think we deserve."
Stephen Chbosky

• DAY 54 •

Weekly Activity: Date Night

One reason I am grateful for my partner is ...

_____

_____

_____

One act of kindness I did for my partner today was ...

_____

_____

_____

One thing my partner has done for me or another today that I mindfully appreciate is ...

_____

_____

_____

> *"Remember that very little is needed to make a happy life;*
> *it is all within yourself in your way of thinking."*
> Marcus Aurelius

• DAY 55 •

Weekly Activity: Date Night

One reason I am grateful for my partner is ...

_____

_____

_____

One act of kindness I did for my partner today was ...

_____

_____

_____

One thing my partner has done for me or another today that I mindfully appreciate is ...

_____

_____

_____

"Knowing is not enough, we must apply;
willing is not enough, we must do."
Bruce Lee

· DAY 56 ·

> **Weekly Activity:** Date Night

One reason I am grateful for my partner is ...

_____

_____

_____

One act of kindness I did for my partner today was ...

_____

_____

_____

One thing my partner has done for me or another today that I mindfully appreciate is ...

_____

_____

_____

> *Piglet: "How do you spell 'love'?"*
> *Winnie the Pooh: "You don't spell it ... you feel it."*
> *A. A. Milne*

Date: _____

• DAY 57 •

Weekly Activity: Date Night

One reason I am grateful for my partner is ...

_____

_____

_____

One act of kindness I did for my partner today was ...

_____

_____

_____

One thing my partner has done for me or another today that I mindfully appreciate is ...

_____

_____

_____

> *"The real potential of in-depth living requires involvement,*
> *by recognizing a need, overcoming fear and taking responsibility.*
> *Watching from the sidelines does not achieve worthwhile goals*
> *and provides little fulfillment."*
> *Peter Shepherd*

95

• DAY 58 •

Weekly Activity: Date Night

One reason I am grateful for my partner is ...

_____

_____

_____

One act of kindness I did for my partner today was ...

_____

_____

_____

One thing my partner has done for me or another today that I mindfully appreciate is ...

_____

_____

_____

"Nobody can go back and start a new beginning,
but anyone can start today to make a new ending."
Maria Robinson

WEEKLY ACTIVITY #9

PASSIONATE TOUCH!
"Kiss Me Like You Mean It"

Every day this week, each partner gets to ask their partner to "kiss me like you mean it" once a day. Since each partner is participating, this will mean a total of two "kiss me like you mean it" kisses a day. The fun here is you can request the kiss at any time in your day, and each one can be different. The only requirement is that it's filled with passion.

Here we bring the meaning back into the kisses. Kissing can be passionate, sensual, intimate, soft, hard, long, short, or whatever you'd like, as long as you fill it with emotion. Kiss like you did on your first date, kiss like you haven't seen your partner in a while, or kiss like it's the last kiss you'll get from them. Whatever this means for you, have fun with it and rise to meet the activity every time a kiss is requested of you. This is a great way to practice intimacy, to reignite the spark, to feel the fire of your relationship.

Long Distance: send each other a picture of you sending a kiss or a description of your kiss when you get your "kiss me like you meant it" request.

Date: _____

• DAY 59 •

Weekly Activity: Kiss Me Like You Mean It

One reason I am grateful for my partner is ...

_____

_____

_____

One act of kindness I did for my partner today was ...

_____

_____

_____

One thing my partner has done for me or another today that I mindfully appreciate is ...

_____

_____

_____

"If there's love in this life we're unstoppable."
*Avicii (*Waiting for Love*)*

• DAY 60 •

Weekly Activity: Kiss Me Like You Mean It

One reason I am grateful for my partner is ...

_____

_____

_____

One act of kindness I did for my partner today was ...

_____

_____

_____

One thing my partner has done for me or another today that I mindfully appreciate is ...

_____

_____

_____

"I think of life itself now as a wonderful play that I've written for myself, and so my purpose is to have the utmost fun playing my part."
Shirley MacLaine

Date: _____

• DAY 61 •

Weekly Activity: Kiss Me Like You Mean It

One reason I am grateful for my partner is ...

_____

_____

_____

One act of kindness I did for my partner today was ...

_____

_____

_____

One thing my partner has done for me or another today that I mindfully appreciate is ...

_____

_____

_____

> *"To the world you may be one person,*
> *but to one person you may be the world."*
> Dr. Seuss

• DAY 62 •

Weekly Activity: Kiss Me Like You Mean It

One reason I am grateful for my partner is ...

_____

_____

_____

One act of kindness I did for my partner today was ...

_____

_____

_____

One thing my partner has done for me or another today that I mindfully appreciate is ...

_____

_____

_____

"By choosing your thoughts, and by selecting which emotional currents you will release and which you will reinforce, you determine the quality of your Light. You determine the effects that you will have on others and the nature of the experiences of your life."
Gary Zukav

• DAY 63 •

Weekly Activity: Kiss Me Like You Mean It

One reason I am grateful for my partner is ...

_____

_____

_____

One act of kindness I did for my partner today was ...

_____

_____

_____

One thing my partner has done for me or another today that I mindfully appreciate is ...

_____

_____

_____

"Life without love is like a tree without blossoms or fruit."
Khalil Gibran

• DAY 64 •

Weekly Activity: Kiss Me Like You Mean It

One reason I am grateful for my partner is ...

_____

_____

_____

One act of kindness I did for my partner today was ...

_____

_____

_____

One thing my partner has done for me or another today that I mindfully appreciate is ...

_____

_____

_____

"Whether you think you can, or think you can't: you're right."
Henry Ford

· DAY 65 ·

Weekly Activity: Kiss Me Like You Mean It

One reason I am grateful for my partner is …

_____

_____

_____

One act of kindness I did for my partner today was …

_____

_____

_____

One thing my partner has done for me or another today that I mindfully appreciate is …

_____

_____

_____

> *"Being defeated is only a temporary condition;*
> *giving up is what makes it permanent."*
> *Marilyn Vos Savant*

WEEKLY ACTIVITY #10

DANCE PARTY!
"Boogie Time"

Put on a song and dance together twice this week—one slow song and one fast song. Dancing is a great way to let loose and show each other unconditional support and love as you each move however your heart desires. Have fun with the different types of songs. This is a "just the two of you" dance party, so if you're already going out dancing this week, still set time apart at home for the two of you to dance.

If dancing together isn't possible because of physical limitations, sit and listen to meaningful music together, really enjoying the time together as you do!

Long Distance: pick your songs and dance it out over facetime/skype.

• DAY 66 •

Weekly Activity: Boogie Time

One reason I am grateful for my partner is ...

_____

_____

_____

One act of kindness I did for my partner today was ...

_____

_____

_____

One thing my partner has done for me or another today that I mindfully appreciate is ...

_____

_____

_____

"Dance like nobody's watching; love like you've never been hurt.
Sing like nobody's listening; live like it's heaven on earth."
Mark Twain

Date: _____

• DAY 67 •

Weekly Activity: Boogie Time

One reason I am grateful for my partner is ...

_____

_____

_____

One act of kindness I did for my partner today was ...

_____

_____

_____

One thing my partner has done for me or another today that I mindfully appreciate is ...

_____

_____

_____

"Any fool can criticize, condemn and complain - and most fools do. But it takes character and self-control to be understanding and forgiving."
Dale Carnegie

107

• DAY 68 •

Weekly Activity: Boogie Time

One reason I am grateful for my partner is ...

_____

_____

_____

One act of kindness I did for my partner today was ...

_____

_____

_____

One thing my partner has done for me or another today that I mindfully appreciate is ...

_____

_____

_____

"The sun shines down, and its image reflects in a thousand different pots filled with water. The reflections are many, but they are each reflecting the same sun. Similarly, when we come to know who we truly are, we will see ourselves in all people."

Amma

• DAY 69 •

Weekly Activity: Boogie Time

One reason I am grateful for my partner is …

_____

_____

_____

One act of kindness I did for my partner today was …

_____

_____

_____

One thing my partner has done for me or another today that I mindfully appreciate is …

_____

_____

_____

"Happiness cannot be traveled to, owned, earned, worn or consumed.
Happiness is the spiritual experience of living every minute
with love, grace, and gratitude."
Denis Waitley

Date: _____

• DAY 70 •

One reason I am grateful for my partner is ...

_____

_____

_____

One act of kindness I did for my partner today was ...

_____

_____

_____

One thing my partner has done for me or another today that I mindfully appreciate is ...

_____

_____

_____

*"Everything can be taken away from a man but one thing:
the last of the human freedoms—to choose one's attitude in
any given set of circumstances, to choose one's own way."*
Viktor Frankl

• DAY 71 •

Weekly Activity: Boogie Time

One reason I am grateful for my partner is ...

_____

_____

_____

One act of kindness I did for my partner today was ...

_____

_____

_____

One thing my partner has done for me or another today that I mindfully appreciate is ...

_____

_____

_____

"I believe empathy is the most essential quality of civilization."
Roger Ebert

· DAY 72 ·

Weekly Activity: Boogie Time

One reason I am grateful for my partner is …

_____

_____

_____

One act of kindness I did for my partner today was …

_____

_____

_____

One thing my partner has done for me or another today that I mindfully appreciate is …

_____

_____

_____

"The best love is the kind that awakens the soul; that makes us reach for more, that plants the fire in our hearts and brings peace to our minds. That's what I hope to give you forever."
Nicholas Sparks

WEEKLY ACTIVITY #11

ASK A FAVOUR!
"Could You Please ..."

Each partner gets to ask their partner for one favour this week. For example, ask for help around the house, doing laundry, making lunches for the kids, doing groceries, etc. A partnership is a constant balancing act, a constant give and take. The more we get comfortable with asking for help and gladly helping each other, the smoother our relationship becomes. When it's your turn to help, see it as a great opportunity to show your partner that you care and that you are always there for them. Complete and ask a favour with love!

Long Distance: the activity remains the same.

· DAY 73 ·

Weekly Activity: Could You Please ...

One reason I am grateful for my partner is ...

_____

_____

_____

One act of kindness I did for my partner today was ...

_____

_____

_____

One thing my partner has done for me or another today that I mindfully appreciate is ...

_____

_____

_____

"Communication is the fuel that keeps the fire of your relationship burning, without it, your relationship goes cold."
William Paisley

Date: _____

• DAY 74 •

One reason I am grateful for my partner is ...

_____

_____

_____

One act of kindness I did for my partner today was ...

_____

_____

_____

One thing my partner has done for me or another today that I mindfully appreciate is ...

_____

_____

_____

*"Have the courage to follow your heart and intuition.
They somehow know what you truly want to become."*
Steve Jobs

Date: _____

• DAY 75 •

> **Weekly Activity:** Could You Please ...

One reason I am grateful for my partner is ...

_____

_____

_____

One act of kindness I did for my partner today was ...

_____

_____

_____

One thing my partner has done for me or another today that I mindfully appreciate is ...

_____

_____

_____

"We are made by love, we are made of love, and we are made for love."
Khurshed Batliwala

• DAY 76 •

Weekly Activity: Could You Please …

One reason I am grateful for my partner is …

_____

_____

_____

One act of kindness I did for my partner today was …

_____

_____

_____

One thing my partner has done for me or another today that I mindfully appreciate is …

_____

_____

_____

"The best thing to hold onto in life is each other"
Audrey Hepburn

Date: _____

• DAY 77 •

Weekly Activity: Could You Please ...

One reason I am grateful for my partner is ...

_____

_____

_____

One act of kindness I did for my partner today was ...

_____

_____

_____

One thing my partner has done for me or another today that I mindfully appreciate is ...

_____

_____

_____

"Love is our true essence. Love has no limitations of caste, religion, race, or nationality. We are all beads strung together on the same thread of love. To awaken this unity—and to spread to others the love that is our inherent nature—is the true goal of human life."

Amma

Date: _____

• DAY 78 •

One reason I am grateful for my partner is …

_____

_____

_____

One act of kindness I did for my partner today was …

_____

_____

_____

One thing my partner has done for me or another today that I mindfully appreciate is …

_____

_____

_____

"The secret of health for both mind and body is not to mourn for the past, worry about the future, or anticipate troubles but to live in the present moment wisely and earnestly."
Buddha

Date: _____

• DAY 79 •

One reason I am grateful for my partner is …

_____

_____

_____

One act of kindness I did for my partner today was …

_____

_____

_____

One thing my partner has done for me or another today that I mindfully appreciate is …

_____

_____

_____

"Do all things with love."
Og Mandino

WEEKLY ACTIVITY #12

COOK A NEW RECIPE!
"Chef Couple"

Have two chefs in the kitchen for one meal this week. Find a new recipe that neither of you has tried and have fun cooking together. Both partners take part in the cooking and in the post-meal cleanup. Cooking together can feel like a date night in the comfort of your own home. Put on some music, let loose, and have fun in the kitchen!

Long distance: pick a recipe, each partner buys the ingredients, and you cook together over facetime/skype.

· DAY 80 ·

Weekly Activity: Chef Couple

One reason I am grateful for my partner is ...

_____

_____

_____

One act of kindness I did for my partner today was ...

_____

_____

_____

One thing my partner has done for me or another today that I mindfully appreciate is ...

_____

_____

_____

> *"The best and most beautiful things in this world cannot be seen or even heard, but must be felt with the heart."*
> Helen Keller

Date: _____

• DAY 81 •

Weekly Activity: Chef Couple

One reason I am grateful for my partner is ...

_____

_____

_____

One act of kindness I did for my partner today was ...

_____

_____

_____

One thing my partner has done for me or another today that I mindfully appreciate is ...

_____

_____

_____

"Compassion is the keen awareness of the interdependence of all things."
Thomas Merton

123

• DAY 82 •

Weekly Activity: Chef Couple

One reason I am grateful for my partner is ...

_____

_____

_____

One act of kindness I did for my partner today was ...

_____

_____

_____

One thing my partner has done for me or another today that I mindfully appreciate is ...

_____

_____

_____

*"As human beings we all want to be happy and free from misery ...
the key to happiness is inner peace. The greatest obstacles to inner peace
are disturbing emotions such as anger, attachment, fear and suspicion,
while love and compassion and a sense of universal responsibility are
the sources of peace and happiness."*
Dalai Lama

• DAY 83 •

Weekly Activity: Chef Couple

One reason I am grateful for my partner is ...

_____

_____

_____

One act of kindness I did for my partner today was ...

_____

_____

_____

One thing my partner has done for me or another today that I mindfully appreciate is ...

_____

_____

_____

"Love is not the opposite of power. Love is power.
Love is the strongest power there is."
Vironika Tugaleva

• DAY 84 •

Weekly Activity: Chef Couple

One reason I am grateful for my partner is...

_____

_____

_____

One act of kindness I did for my partner today was...

_____

_____

_____

One thing my partner has done for me or another today that I mindfully appreciate is...

_____

_____

_____

"Love is what we were born with. Fear is what we have learned here. The spiritual journey is the relinquishment - or unlearning - of fear and the acceptance of love back into our hearts. Love is our ultimate reality and our purpose on earth. To be consciously aware of it, to experience love in ourselves and others, is the meaning of life."
Marianne Williamson

• DAY 85 •

> **Weekly Activity:** Chef Couple

One reason I am grateful for my partner is …

_____

_____

_____

One act of kindness I did for my partner today was …

_____

_____

_____

One thing my partner has done for me or another today that I mindfully appreciate is …

_____

_____

_____

"Life is not discovery of fate; it is continuous creation of future, through choices of thoughts and actions in the present."
Sanjay Sahay

Date: _____

• DAY 86 •

One reason I am grateful for my partner is ...

_____

_____

_____

One act of kindness I did for my partner today was ...

_____

_____

_____

One thing my partner has done for me or another today that I mindfully appreciate is ...

_____

_____

_____

"We must not allow the clock and the calendar to blind us to the fact that each moment of life is a miracle and mystery."
H. G. Wells

WEEKLY ACTIVITY #13

RELAX WITH A MASSAGE!
"Caring Touch"

Give your partner a five-plus-minute massage of their choosing. Decide on a length of time that suits you both and give each other a massage on separate days this week. Why separate days? So that your partner's massage is all about making them happy and vice versa. When it's your turn to massage, pamper your partner. Let the massage be the way you show them just how special they are. When it's your turn to receive, enjoy it fully. Indulge.

Long Distance: get creative! Describe your caring touch to each other or share something that touches your partner's heart (poem, song, passage from a book). Give each other a touching five minutes on separate days.

• DAY 87 •

Weekly Activity: Caring Touch

One reason I am grateful for my partner is …

_____

_____

_____

One act of kindness I did for my partner today was …

_____

_____

_____

One thing my partner has done for me or another today that I mindfully appreciate is …

_____

_____

_____

> *"I love you, not only for what you are but for*
> *what I am when I am with you."*
> Roy Croft

• DAY 88 •

Weekly Activity: Caring Touch

One reason I am grateful for my partner is ...

_____

_____

_____

One act of kindness I did for my partner today was ...

_____

_____

_____

One thing my partner has done for me or another today that I mindfully appreciate is ...

_____

_____

_____

*"Those who bring sunshine into the lives of others
cannot keep it from themselves."*
J.M. Barrie

• DAY 89 •

Weekly Activity: Caring Touch

One reason I am grateful for my partner is ...

_____

_____

_____

One act of kindness I did for my partner today was ...

_____

_____

_____

One thing my partner has done for me or another today that I mindfully appreciate is ...

_____

_____

_____

"Yesterday I was clever, so I wanted to change the world.
Today I am wise, so I am changing myself."
Rumi

• DAY 90 •

One reason I am grateful for my partner is ...

_____

_____

_____

One act of kindness I did for my partner today was ...

_____

_____

_____

One thing my partner has done for me or another today that I mindfully appreciate is ...

_____

_____

_____

"I love you without knowing how, or when, or from where.
I love you simply, without problems or pride: I love you in this way
because I do not know any other way of loving but this, in which there is
no I or you, so intimate that your hand upon my chest is my hand,
so intimate that when I fall asleep your eyes close."
Pablo Neruda

Date: _____

• DAY 91 •

One reason I am grateful for my partner is ...

_____

_____

_____

One act of kindness I did for my partner today was ...

_____

_____

_____

One thing my partner has done for me or another today that I mindfully appreciate is ...

_____

_____

_____

"Love one another and help others to rise to the higher levels, simply by pouring out love. Love is infectious and the greatest healing energy."
Sai Baba

• DAY 92 •

> **Weekly Activity:** Caring Touch

One reason I am grateful for my partner is ...

_____

_____

_____

One act of kindness I did for my partner today was ...

_____

_____

_____

One thing my partner has done for me or another today that I mindfully appreciate is ...

_____

_____

_____

"It's the repetition of affirmations that leads to belief, and once that belief becomes a firm conviction, things begin to happen."
Claude M. Bristol

• DAY 93 •

Weekly Activity: Caring Touch

One reason I am grateful for my partner is ...

_____

_____

_____

One act of kindness I did for my partner today was ...

_____

_____

_____

One thing my partner has done for me or another today that I mindfully appreciate is ...

_____

_____

_____

"The object of love is not getting something you want but doing something for the well-being of the one you love."
Gary Chapman

WEEKLY ACTIVITY #14

STORY TIME!
"I Fell in Love Because ..."

Take turns telling each other how and why you fell in love with each other. Take some time to reflect on all the reasons you fell for your partner and how your relationship has grown. You both know how you met, so think about those special details, the personality traits, the things that stood out to you and made them stand apart. Think of all the truthful details you know will be meaningful to your partner and be open to sharing. Once you've had time to reflect, take turns lovingly exchanging your stories of how and why you fell in love.

Long Distance: the activity remains the same.

Date: _____

• DAY 94 •

One reason I am grateful for my partner is …

_____

_____

_____

One act of kindness I did for my partner today was …

_____

_____

_____

One thing my partner has done for me or another today that I mindfully appreciate is …

_____

_____

_____

"Kind words can be short and easy to speak,
but their echoes are truly endless."
Mother Theresa

• DAY 95 •

Weekly Activity: I Fell in Love Because …

One reason I am grateful for my partner is …

_____

_____

_____

One act of kindness I did for my partner today was …

_____

_____

_____

One thing my partner has done for me or another today that I mindfully appreciate is …

_____

_____

_____

"Trust is all about fearing less and loving more."
Unknown

Date: _____

• DAY 96 •

One reason I am grateful for my partner is …

_____

_____

_____

One act of kindness I did for my partner today was …

_____

_____

_____

One thing my partner has done for me or another today that I mindfully appreciate is …

_____

_____

_____

"You create your own reality and take personal responsibility for it. Your life is a reflection of who you are and the experiences that you, as a soul, planned for this life."
Owen Waters

Date: _____

• DAY 97 •

Weekly Activity: I Fell in Love Because …

One reason I am grateful for my partner is …

_____

_____

_____

One act of kindness I did for my partner today was …

_____

_____

_____

One thing my partner has done for me or another today that I mindfully appreciate is …

_____

_____

_____

"The greatness of a man is not in how much wealth he acquires, but in his integrity and his ability to affect those around him positively."
Bob Marley

141

Date: _____

• DAY 98 •

One reason I am grateful for my partner is …

_____

_____

_____

One act of kindness I did for my partner today was …

_____

_____

_____

One thing my partner has done for me or another today that I mindfully appreciate is …

_____

_____

_____

"When there is love in your heart,
everything outside of you also becomes lovable."
Veeresh

Date: _____

• DAY 99 •

| **Weekly Activity:** I Fell in Love Because … |

One reason I am grateful for my partner is …

_____

_____

_____

One act of kindness I did for my partner today was …

_____

_____

_____

One thing my partner has done for me or another today that I mindfully appreciate is …

_____

_____

_____

> "The only way love can last a lifetime is if it's unconditional.
> The truth is this: love is not determined by the one being loved,
> but rather by the one choosing to love."
> Stephen Kendrick

Date: _____

• DAY 100 •

One reason I am grateful for my partner is ...

_____

_____

_____

One act of kindness I did for my partner today was ...

_____

_____

_____

One thing my partner has done for me or another today that I mindfully appreciate is ...

_____

_____

_____

"We are all we need."
Above & Beyond

144

A LETTER TO MY LOVE

A Reflection of the Last 100 Days

_____

_____

_____

_____

_____

_____

_____

_____

_____

_____

_____

_____

_____

_____

THANK YOU!

We are overwhelmingly grateful that you took this journey with us, and we send an endless amount of love from our partnership to yours!

We wish you all the happiness in the world—the kind of happiness that comes from never-ending growth and the discovery of new levels of fulfilment each day.

Help us spread the love. Please leave us a review and share your journey with us on Facebook and Instagram @LovingPartnerJournal We'd love to hear and see how it went!

Share this journal with anyone who would enjoy deepening their love.

We're all in this together after all!
May your love run deep
and your light shine bright.

Love, Josh and Lauren

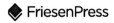 FriesenPress

Suite 300 - 990 Fort St
Victoria, BC, V8V 3K2
Canada

www.friesenpress.com

Copyright © 2018 by Lauren and Joshua Graham
First Edition — 2018

www.LovingPartnerJournal.com
Facebook & Instagram:
@lovingpartnerjournal

Disclaimer:
This book is not intended as a substitute for professional opinion. This book is designed to provide information and motivation to our readers. It is sold with the understanding that the publisher and author are not engaged to render any type of psychological, legal, or other kind of professional advice. Neither the publisher nor the authors shall be liable for any physical, psychological, emotional, financial, or commercial damages, including, but not limited to, special, incidental, consequential, or other damages. Our views and rights are the same: You are responsible for your own choices, actions, and results.

ISBN
978-1-5255-2540-7 (Hardcover)
978-1-5255-2541-4 (Paperback)

1. FAMILY & RELATIONSHIPS, MARRIAGE

Distributed to the trade by The Ingram Book Company

CPSIA information can be obtained
at www.ICGtesting.com
Printed in the USA
LVOW11s0358230618
581448LV00001BA/13/P